CW00758449

THOMAS N HUFFMAN

MAPUNGUBWE

ANCIENT AFRICAN CIVILISATION ON THE LIMPOPO

WITS UNIVERSITY PRESS

Please remember that without an official permit visitors, including archaeologists,
are not allowed to remove artefacts from any site within the basin.

Wits University Press
1 Jan Smuts Avenue
Johannesburg
2001
South Africa

http://witspress.wits.ac.za

ISBN 1-86814-408-9

Cover by Limeblue, Johannesburg, South Africa
Text design by Orchard Publishing, Cape Town,
  South Africa
Printed and bound by Creda Communications
  Cape Town, South Africa

CONTENTS

ACKNOWLEDGEMENTS

I am indebted to John Calabrese, McEdward Murimbika, Alex Schoeman, Jeannette Smith and Marilee Wood for the use of their research results. Lance Gewer of Icon Productions made available Lance Penny's artist impressions of Mapungubwe on pages 32, 33 and 40. Johan Delannoie created the impression of K2 on page 18 and the drawing of Mapungubwe on the cover. Bob Cnoops photographed these reconstructions as well as the artefacts on pages 11, 20, 21, 48 and 49. Wendy Voorvelt prepared the maps. Marilee Wood provided the photograph of the beads on page 21. The Mapungubwe Archives, University of Pretoria, kindly supplied the photographs on pages 19, 34, 39, 47 and 53, and gave their permission to use the material on pages 35, 36 and 47 from the edited volume on Mapungubwe by Fouche 1937. The figure on page 38 comes from Gardner 1963. The National Culture History Museum Pretoria gave permission to use the photograph on page 11. The aerial photograph on page 31 is courtesy of the Trigonometrical Survey of South Africa. Finally, I am grateful to the various organizations that have supported our research in the Mapungubwe area, in particular De Beers, the Mellon Foundation, the Indigenous Knowledge Systems of the National Research Foundation, SANParks and the University of the Witwatersrand.

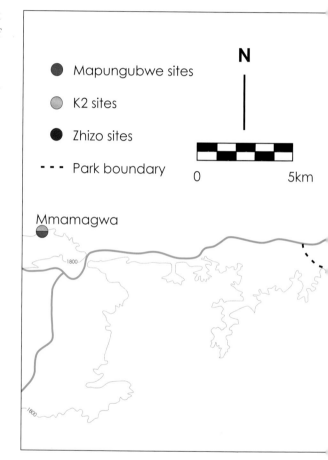

▲ Location of the Mapungubwe Park and important sites

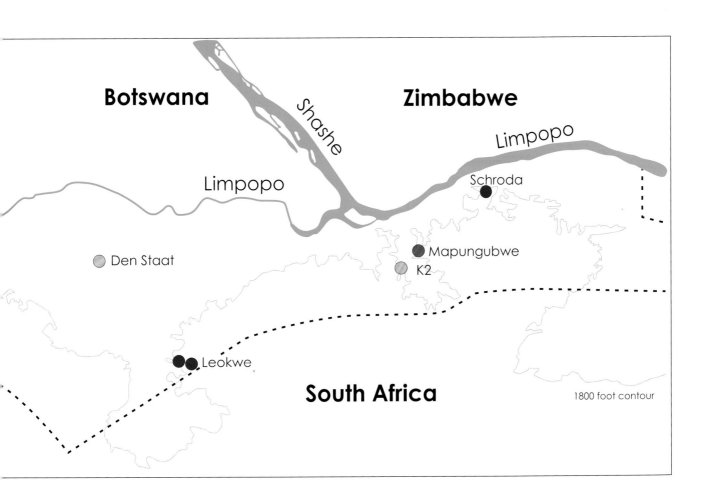

OCCUPATION OF THE SHASHE-LIMPOPO BASIN

List of the important places and events in their chronological order.

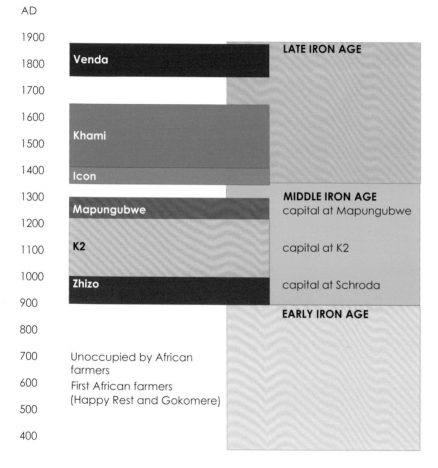

AD

1900	
1800	Venda — LATE IRON AGE
1700	
1600	
1500	Khami
1400	Icon
1300	Mapungubwe — MIDDLE IRON AGE, capital at Mapungubwe
1200	
1100	K2 — capital at K2
1000	Zhizo — capital at Schroda
900	EARLY IRON AGE
800	
700	Unoccupied by African farmers
600	First African farmers (Happy Rest and Gokomere)
500	
400	

INTRODUCTION

Between AD 900 and 1300, a period known as the Middle Iron Age, African people in the Shashe-Limpopo basin developed the first complex society in southern Africa. Characterised by sacred leadership and distinct social classes, this society also created the first town, the first king, the first stone-walled palace and the capital of the first state. Because of these firsts, the Mapungubwe Cultural Landscape (also known as the Mapungubwe National Park) has become one of South Africa's World Heritage listings. This international status recognises the importance of Mapungubwe to the African past.

The World Heritage area is a remarkable example of a prehistoric cultural landscape, as recent settlement has not disturbed the most important sites. Indeed, each of the three capitals represents a separate slice of time – first Schroda (AD 900–1000), then K2 (1000–1220) and finally Mapungubwe itself (1220–1300). Furthermore, many ordinary homesteads have not been disturbed, except by natural forces, since the time they were abandoned. As a result, archaeologists have been able to reconstruct the changing uses of the landscape during the rise of Mapungubwe.

Mapungubwe was the forerunner of the famous town of Great Zimbabwe, another World Heritage site about 200 kilometres away. Indeed, without the earlier events and developments in the Shashe-Limpopo basin, Great Zimbabwe would not have existed. By the 15th century, the type of society developed at Mapungubwe had spread over an area the size of France.

What is more, essentially the same type of society lives on today in Venda, although a direct genetic link does not exist. Mapungubwe people are gone, but the culture is by no means dead.

Because of this cultural connection to Great Zimbabwe and then the Venda people, it is possible to use historical and traditional evidence to understand the evolution of Mapungubwe. The story begins over 1000 years ago and involves the wildlife and geography of the area, as well as its people.

GEOLOGY AND CLIMATE

The Shashe-Limpopo basin lies in what geologists call the Limpopo Mobile Belt between two ancient continents, the Zimbabwe craton and the Kaapvaal craton (South Africa). Granite forms the two cratons to the north and south, while erosion over many millions of years has produced the sandstones in the basin. As the continents moved, cracks appeared in the earth's crust, allowing magma to come up from the earth's core to form basalt sheets and dolerite dykes. One impressive dyke standing near Mapungubwe looks like a man-made wall.

Over time, the Limpopo River in the centre of the belt changed course, creating the escarpment to the west of Mapungubwe. More recent fluvial terraces cover the valley floor. In the time of Mapungubwe, the Limpopo itself flowed permanently, but the Shashe was a river of sand with water underneath. When the Shashe occasionally floods, it acts as a dam wall and backs up the Limpopo for several kilometres. The short but narrow gorge downstream of the confluence enhances the dam effect, and depending on rainfall, flooding would have been a regular occurrence. In fact, during the Middle Iron Age, the Limpopo was the Nile of Southern Africa.

The climate would have supported dense forests with ilala palms (*Hyphaene natalensis*) alongside the riverbanks. Though the forests have now mostly disappeared, the floodplains still support saltbush (*Salvadora angustifolia*) where the soils overlie basalt, while mopane trees (*Colophospermum mopane*) grow elsewhere in the valley and on the plateau above.

All these natural features played a part in the rise of Mapungubwe.

▲ Looking north across the Shashe-Limpopo confluence

▶ Typical sandstone koppie (left) and dolerite dyke (right)

SCHRODA

The capital

African farmers were absent from the Shashe-Limpopo basin between about AD 600 and 900, because the climate was not suitable. At this time, Zhizo people (named after their characteristic pottery)* lived in better-watered areas in southwest Zimbabwe and eastern Botswana. Some Zhizo people moved south from Zimbabwe in about AD 900 and established a settlement at Schroda, near the banks of the Limpopo. Cattle dung and domestic animal bones show that they herded cattle and small stock, while grindstones, the burnt remains of grain bins and the shapes and sizes of their pottery attest to farming. The size of the settlement suggests that some 300–500 people lived there.

▲ Excavations in the chief's area at Schroda, with the Limpopo in the background

Schroda – taken from the name of the form – was the largest Zhizo settlement in the basin at the time, which indicates that it was the capital. Throughout southern Africa, settlement size was related to male political power. As a rule, the chief was the wealthiest person in the chiefdom, accumulating more cattle than anyone else through court fines, forfeits, tributes, raids and the high bride price of his daughters. Because of this wealth, the chief had more wives, more fields, more followers and more court officials – and therefore the largest settlement.

* Different groups of people produced different pottery styles, and by convention, the people are named after the pottery. Pre-historic pottery styles are named after the first place they were found.

Figurines

In the recent past chiefs usually controlled the rites of passage in their societies, such as female initiations. In Southern Africa, female initiations often involved the use of figurines as props in lessons taught through metaphor and symbol during the school. Archaeological excavations at Schroda uncovered a large cache of unusual figurines that were probably used in a similar school. This cache includes animals, humans and creatures of fantasy. They were found next to the main cattle kraal: finely made domestic animals lay broken and discarded on one side of a wooden fence, while roughly made animals and fantasy creatures lay on the other. This division probably had something to do with the lessons. Generally speaking, the lessons would have covered such topics as the history of the group, various aspects of social organisation and proper moral behaviour.

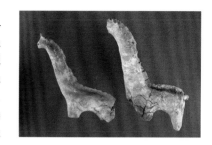

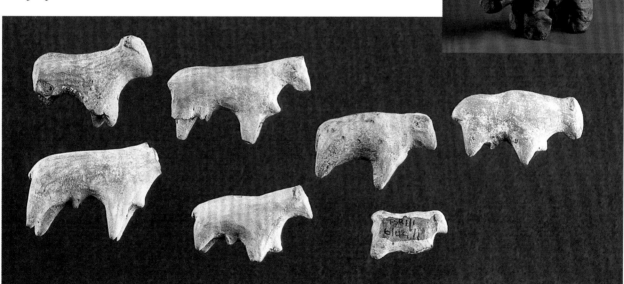

▲ Wild animals and fantasy creatures in the figurine cache at Schroda
▶ Domestic animal figurines in the cache at Schroda

Elephants and settlements

Until a few years ago, archaeologists thought that Zhizo communities had moved into the Shashe-Limpopo basin because the climate had become wetter than it is today. Newer climatic evidence, however, shows that rainfall did not improve until the K2 period, around AD 1000. It was elephant ivory, not agriculture, that was the attraction. An ivory trade with the East African coast existed in Zimbabwe for about 100 years before Zhizo people entered the basin. As the thriving herds today demonstrate, the basin is prime elephant country, and elephants probably lived throughout the area.

The high number of elephants in the basin probably explains the distribution of Zhizo settlements. Most were located well away from the rivers and floodplains because otherwise elephants would have destroyed the fields. (Until recently, this was the problem with agriculture in the Maramani Communal Area across the river in Zimbabwe.) The artefacts from Schroda also demonstrate an ivory trade. Schroda, in fact, is the first settlement in the basin to yield a large amount of ivory working debris.

Botswana

Mmamagwa

▶ Distribution of Zhizo settlement in the basin. Most settlements were located some distance from good agricultural lands.

12

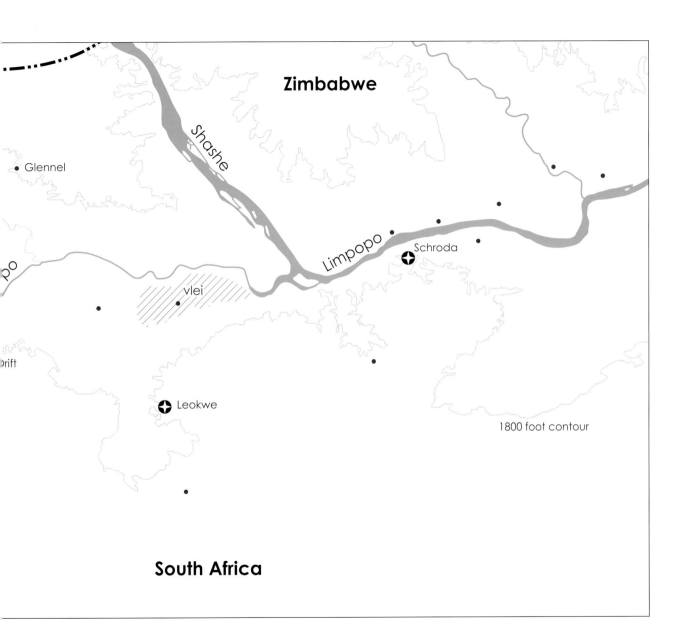

Zimbabwe

Shashe

Glennel

Limpopo

vlei

Schroda

Drift

Leokwe

1800 foot contour

South Africa

International trade

Besides ivory debris, excavations at Schroda also uncovered a large quantity of exotic glass beads. These beads show that the Indian Ocean ivory trade had reached Southern Africa by this time. Later Portuguese accounts describe how the trade followed the rhythms of the monsoons. Such goods as ivory, gold, rhino horn, leopard skins and iron were taken from the interior to coastal stations in Mozambique, such as Sofala (in what is now the Bazaruto area), where Arab/Swahili dhows transported them up the coast to the most powerful Arab/Swahili city, Mogadishu.

After the goods were taxed, traders sailed on the easterly monsoon winds to Arabia and India. There they exchanged the African goods for such items as glass beads, cotton and silk cloths, and glazed ceramics. On the reverse monsoon, the traders returned to Mogadishu, where they were taxed again, before sailing down the coast to Sofala to begin another cycle. Zhizo people controlled the Shashe-Limpopo portion of this trade for about 100 years.

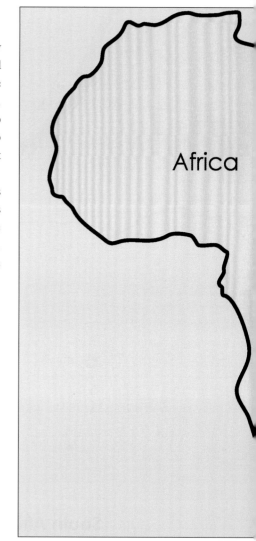

▶ Trade routes in the Indian Ocean network

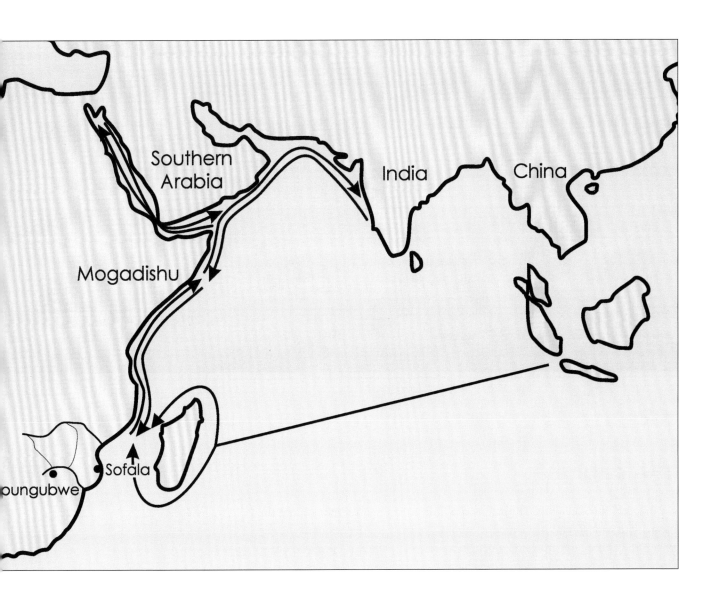

K2

The capital

Around AD 1000, Leopard's Kopje people from further south moved into the basin. The widespread replacement of Zhizo pottery by the Leopard's Kopje style shows that Leopard's Kopje people took over the area. The Zhizo chiefdom moved west into Botswana and abandoned the basin altogether.

Because they have disappeared from the archaeological record, we do not know what language Zhizo people spoke (other than a division of the Bantu

language family, like all other Iron Age people in southern Africa). On the other hand, Leopard's Kopje pottery can be traced into more recent times, and that is how we know that Leopard's Kopje people spoke an early form of Shona, the major language family in Zimbabwe today. More specifically, they would have spoken Kalanga – that is, Western Shona.

K2 was the Leopard's Kopje capital – the largest settlement in its day. By the beginning of the thirteenth century, some 1500 people sheltered under its roofs. On the basis of many historical examples in southern Africa, archaeologists believe the K2 capital would have been organised into several residential areas, each under the immediate authority of a family head or ward headman. The largest division belonged to the chief.

Chief's residential area

The centre of the K2 capital is now marked by a large hole excavated in the 1930s. These excavations uncovered numerous house remains sited in between grain bins and middens (household refuse dumps) at the back and a large cattle kraal in front. On the basis of a widespread settlement organisation known as the Central Cattle Pattern, we believe the chief probably lived on the western edge of this residential complex. His wives and children, adult sons and their families and other relatives and friends probably occupied the other houses.

Typically, the houses consisted of circular *daga* (a mixture of mud and dung) walls with red gravel and white clay floors, all covered by a thatched roof. Some houses probably had verandas. Recent settlement patterns again suggest that different kinds of structures served different functions. Thus, married women had their own kitchen, fathers had their own sleeping room, and bachelor boys and girls slept in separate huts near the front of the residential zone.

Throughout the Eastern Bantu-speaking world, societies that arranged houses around a central cattle kraal also emphasised a symbolic relationship between women, houses and graves. As elsewhere, then, the main residential area at K2 would have belonged to the domain of women.

▲ Artist's reconstruction of the chief's area at the beginning of K2. Note houses and grain bins.

Burials

Excavations in the 1930s uncovered over 90 graves in the female residential zone. Most were of women and children, buried in a flexed position, and many faced west. These features conform to a widespread pattern of burials that still has resonance today. As a rule, people should be buried in settlement areas that were associated with them in life. Married women, for example, should be buried in the private space behind their house, children in the front courtyard where they used to play, infants under the house where they were born and men in or near the cattle kraal. Furthermore, men should be buried lying on their right-hand side, the senior side, and women lying on their left. These rules are not as strong for children because they were too young to follow the rules when they were alive. Everyone, however, should be placed in a sleeping position because death is part of a cycle and therefore temporary.

▲ Child burial at K2. Note the flexed, 'sleeping' posture.

Normal deaths should also point west, towards sunset, the direction symbolically associated with death. Abnormal deaths might not follow these rules. Some later Mapungubwe period graves, for example, were dug into the large midden next to the cattle kraal. These people could have died under strange circumstances and required unusual treatment.

Archaeologists today treat human burials with great respect. In some cases, the skeletons are reburied after they have been studied.

Copper and iron working

Excavations in the female residential zone have yielded the remains of copper working, such as copper slag, fragments of copper crucibles and fragments of clay blowpipes. Copper melts at a relatively low temperature, but it must be reduced in some kind of furnace. Blowpipes attached to bellows help the coppersmith to reach the required temperatures. The copper is then manufactured into beads, bangles and other ornaments.

The copper ore must have come from outside the basin, because the local geology is devoid of all metals. There are good copper deposits near Musina, which is the closest source, and some were exploited in pre-colonial times.

In many parts of Africa there is a symbolic association between the colour of copper and women. Locally, some societies use copper bangles as the focal point for rituals involving female ancestors. Because of this association, copper was probably melted in the residential zone behind the houses.

Iron, on the other hand, is associated with men. A male ancestor would have a specially made spear as his focal point for rituals. We believe that K2 people followed this pattern. Like copper, iron ore must have come from outside the basin, perhaps from the Tswapong Hills in Botswana about 100 kilometres away, or from Dongola Mountain to the east. Remains of iron furnaces have not yet been found anywhere in the basin, but fragments of iron objects are common in the capitals. K2 itself has yielded some 75 pieces of iron bangles, round and square wire, beads, pendants and a remarkable knife with an ivory handle.

▲ Copper bracelet from K2
◀ Iron knife with ivory handle from K2

Ivory and glass beads

Excavations at K2 have yielded huge quantities of ivory objects, from complete tusks through finished bracelets to chips. Some of the finished items were probably meant for local consumption because ivory bracelets were important signs of status throughout Southern Africa. Long half-bracelets may have been wrist guards for special archers, perhaps men who formed an honour guard for the chief. Some of the ivory was destined for Arabia, to become the hilts on knives given to young men after circumcision. In Southern Africa, ivory working was a male activity that took place in the men's area near the cattle kraal. Ivory workers at K2 discarded their debris in the large midden next to the main kraal.

Excavations in this midden in the 1930s yielded thousands of glass beads. Many ranged in colour from blue through turquoise to green. K2 craftsmen made some of these into a larger type called 'garden rollers' – named after a garden implement. Archaeologists have found the clay moulds in the midden, and presumably men made the beads in the men's area. Garden rollers are the product of the first and only local bead industry on record. Perhaps the trade brought so many beads into the basin that the leaders had them combined into larger items to maintain their value. These home-made beads have been found surprisingly far away; for example on the edge of the Makgadikgadi Pans 350 kilometres to the northwest, and 450 kilometres to the southwest beyond Gaborone. Evidently K2 had an extensive network of connections in the interior, and its leader was a powerful man.

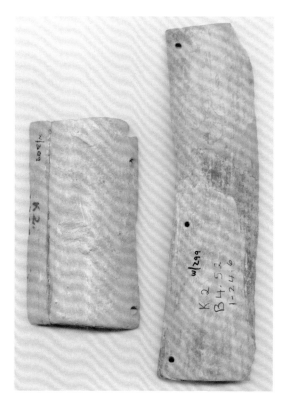

▲ Ivory objects from K2. Archers may have used these as wrist guards.

◀ Garden roller beads and moulds from K2. These unique items were made from smaller imported beads.

Court, kraal and midden

Throughout southern Africa, the men's court belonged to the leader of the settlement. The amount of court activity depended on his political standing. Family heads, for example, resolved disputes within their homestead, but disputes between different homesteads, or different neighbourhoods and districts, went to a higher court. Besides acting as the highest court of appeal, the chief's court heard cases that affected the nation, such as witchcraft. On other formal occasions, men arranged marriages or pursued other political activities. At informal times, men worked ivory and skins and generally spent their leisure time there. At the time of K2, the court was always near the cattle kraal.

▼ A modern cattle kraal, showing build-up of dung

The central cattle kraal was the other principal component of the men's domain. Men were buried in or near the cattle kraal, and cattle were the best sacrifice to male ancestors. Furthermore, payment of the bride price in cattle, commonly called *lobola*, was and still is one of the most important social institutions in Southern Africa. The central cattle kraal, therefore, was extremely important. Two thick dung layers mark this kraal at K2. Both layers contain several thin white horizontal lines that represent crust surfaces made by cattle. Usually, a cattle kraal has one crust surface that was formed at the bottom when cattle first used the pen. The multiple crust surfaces at K2 are probably the result of sporadic use because cattle would not stay in a chief's kraal for long.

The bones of cattle slaughtered as payment for a transgression form part of a midden associated with the court. Young men swept up the ash from the men's fireplaces, broken pots from beer drinks, and other debris from male activities and dumped them in this special midden. Normal household refuse was not dumped here, but in small middens behind the residential units. Excavations through the K2 midden revealed alternating layers of ash and bone. The angle of these layers shows that the top, or tops, shifted over time. Ultimately, the midden reached a height of four metres above the ground.

◀ Cattle dung from the central area at K2. Note the many thin white lines representing successive kraal floors.

▲ The central midden at K2. Note the angle of the multiple ash layers. Among other things, this midden yielded enormous quantities of cattle bones.

Commoners

Many K2 people lived in small homesteads away from the capital. These small homesteads (60–80 metres in diameter) followed the organisational principles of the Central Cattle Pattern. As in the capital, the centre was the domain of men. Here the cattle kraal would be found, where men related by blood and other important people were buried, and a court, where men resolved disputes and made political decisions. This male area could also include sunken grain pits for long-term storage. The outer residential zone, the female domain, incorporated the households of married women, each with its own kitchen, sleeping house, grain bins and graves. Good examples exist on the farm Den Staat. The cattle kraal in one homestead there burnt at such a high temperature that the silica in the dung vitrified (that is, it turned to glass), forming a low hard mound.

These small homesteads would have been grouped into neighbourhoods, each under the immediate authority of a headman. In contrast to the Zhizo period, the majority were located next to the Limpopo floodplains. A favoured area was along the edge of the Kolope delta, where the small stream tried to work its way to the Limpopo. This new location shows that K2 people were now cultivating the rich agricultural soils, and the remains of numerous grain bins demonstrate their success. Some granaries

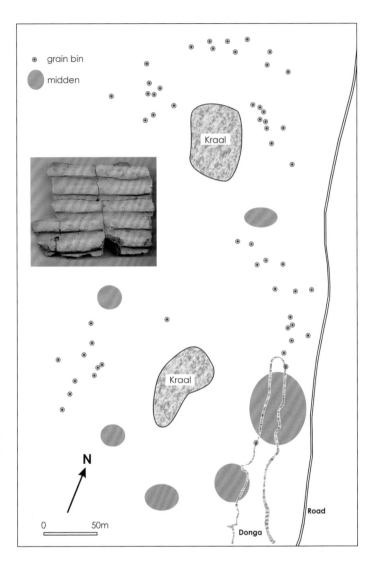

▲ Plan of two K2-period homesteads on Den Staat with the Central Cattle Pattern. Inset is a fragment of a decorated grain bin.

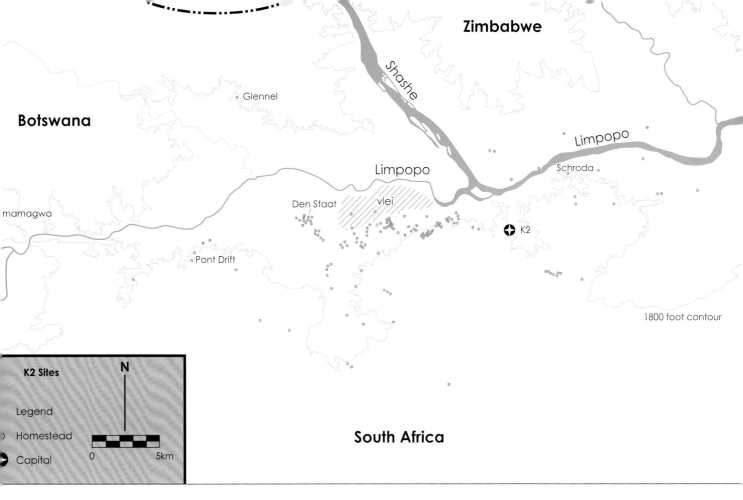

Distribution of K2-period homesteads in the Shashe-Limpopo basin. Most are located along the edge of the floodplains.

were decorated with parallel, horizontal grooves. Similar decoration in the nineteenth century referred to a symbolic association between women and agriculture.

Excavations around the granaries revealed several small storage pits that were probably used for root crops. These would have been only slightly sealed, and the first rains would wash soil into the pits, causing the plants to produce sprouts that could be planted for a new crop.

Agriculture

Carbonised grains show that K2 people cultivated sorghum, pearl millet, finger millet, ground beans and cowpeas. Fields probably also included calabashes. All these crops have African origins, and the first Iron Age farmers brought them to Southern Africa. The African cereals have varying requirements, but generally, the minimum annual rainfall needs to be about 500 mm. This is at least 100 mm higher than today. According to recent climatic data, annual rainfall increased to this level some time during the K2 period.

▲ Locations of agricultural settlements in the foreground; rich floodplains in the background

Increased rainfall would have contributed to increased flooding. Floodplains are good choices for traditional agriculture because they can hold more water and for longer periods than other soils. In some cases it might be possible to produce a cereal crop from floodwaters alone, especially because some varieties of sorghum and millets are adapted to moister conditions. Furthermore, if the high rainfall after AD 1000 extended the rainy season, then the warm temperatures that characterise the basin could have also extended the growing season.

The population in the basin expanded during the K2 period, both on the land and in the capital. This expansion would have had its impact on agricultural production. According to later historical records, food for the capital came from specially designated fields rather than from an individual farmer's own surplus. Everyone, including residents of the capital, would have helped to cultivate these fields as a form of tribute.

Rainmaking

Rainmaking is still widely practised in southern Africa, but it remains a sacred and secretive ritual. We know that rainmaking is a cyclical process coupled with agricultural activities, rather than an isolated event, and that chiefs themselves are in charge, even though they are usually not rainmakers. At the start of the rainy season, between September and November, rainmakers conduct rituals using medicines to summon the clouds. Next, the people start to work in the tribute field before clearing their own. At the end of the season, the chief leads a harvest celebration that can be quite elaborate, involving dancing and beer made from the tribute grain.

▲ A typical rainmaking hill in the Shashe-Limpopo basin

In the Shashe-Limpopo basin, a certain kind of hill was used during the rainmaking cycle. These hills have steep sides with difficult access for cattle, insufficient space for a normal homestead and man-made dolly holes, or more shallow cupules, in association with natural cisterns and natural rock pools. Excavations have uncovered sorghum that would have been used to make ritual beer, as well as pottery for producing and consuming the beer. K2 pottery is present in all known cases.

Chiefs sometimes hired strangers as rainmakers. These strangers could be 'first peoples' – that is, people who were there before and who therefore had a special relationship with the ancient spirits of the land. San hunter-gatherers, for example, are known to have played this role.

Ethnicity

To present-day anthropologists, ethnicity involves the interplay between minorities and dominant groups within the same political system. The ethnic groups themselves consist of people who form a limited social and historical entity, distinct from other similar entities through such aspects as customs, beliefs and material culture.

The Shashe-Limpopo basin provides the earliest known example of ethnic interaction between African farmers in southern Africa. Ceramic evidence shows that some Zhizo people stayed behind (or returned later) after K2 took over the basin. Their ceramic style (now called Leokwe after the hill where the pottery was first found.) changed in a few details as a result of interaction with K2, but it was clearly derived from Zhizo.

▲ Leokwe Hill. Leokwe people were an ethnic minority during the K2 period.

An older Zhizo community had lived on the south side of Leokwe Hill, and then later, when K2 was the capital, Leokwe people established a village on the north side. Since the capital is only a few kilometres away, the Leokwe village must have owed allegiance to K2.

To K2, Leokwe represented 'first peoples' with a special relationship to the spirits of the land. Leokwe Hill itself may have been a rainmaking site, and the Leokwe people may have therefore been ritual specialists, such as rainmakers and diviners.

Evidently, Leokwe people also herded cattle for K2 people. There are several places where 'extra' cattle kraals lie between Leokwe homesteads. One such complex lies in the secluded canyon that houses the Main Rest Camp. This canyon, only two kilometres from the K2 capital, has permanent water and access to the mopane plateau. Cattle browse on mopane trees in winter, and so the mopane veld was an important resource to herdsmen in the past.

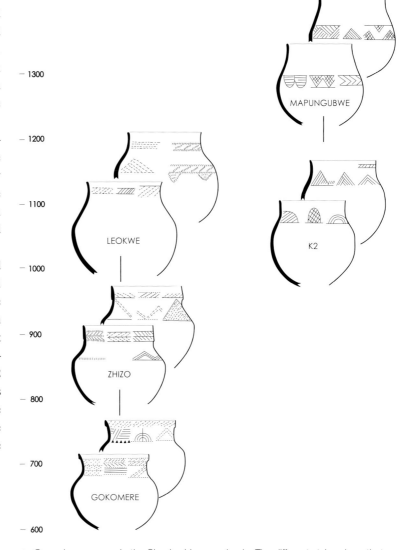

▲ Ceramic sequence in the Shashe-Limpopo basin. The different styles show that Leokwe and K2 were separate groups of people.

29

Social changes

K2 was the capital for about 200 years, from AD 1000 to 1220. During this long time, the spatial organisation of the settlement changed: cattle were moved away from the centre, and the court midden was allowed to cover the old kraal.

In later historical times, in the Zimbabwe culture, cattle were more or less royal property, and there were two courts, one for royalty and another for commoners. Furthermore, the commoners' court was not associated with cattle. Assuming that this pattern had evolved at K2, the shift of the kraal probably indicates that cattle were no longer a medium to bind everyone together and that the central court had become a place only for commoners. Social ranking was becoming more distinct.

The development of formal class structures probably came about through two main factors: trade and agriculture. The enormous wealth generated through the Indian Ocean trade resulted in an unprecedented inequality, and ruling families became an upper class. In addition, a growing population, supported by floodplain agriculture, would have helped to intensify the existing social differences. By AD 1220, K2 society had transformed from one based on social ranking to one based on social classes.

When K2 was first established, its spatial arrangement would have paralleled social ranking, but 200 years later, when social classes had evolved, the pattern needed to be changed to keep in step. K2 people then moved to Mapungubwe.

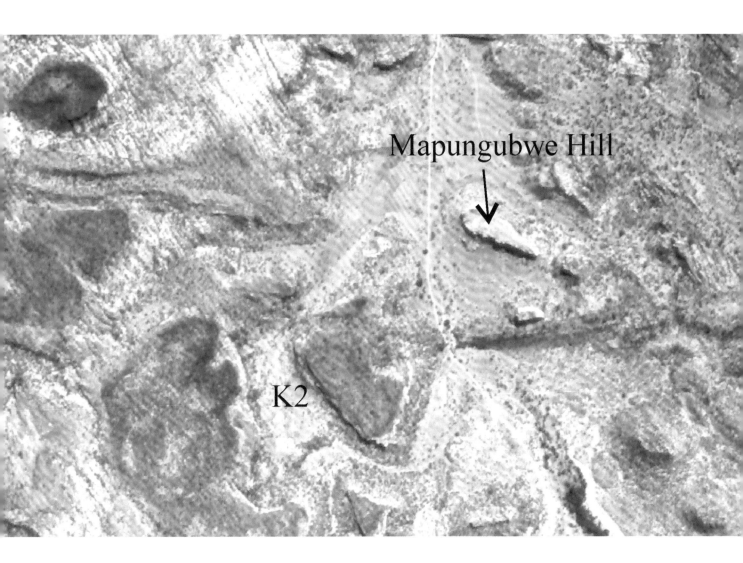

Mapungubwe Hill

K2

▲ Aerial view of K2 and Mapungubwe

MAPUNGUBWE

When Mapungubwe became the capital, in about AD 1220, most people set-
tled below the hill and in front of it – that is, on the west side. The commoners'
court was established at the base of the hill next to the tall boulder, and cattle
were not associated with it. From the beginning of this new occupation, a few
elite people lived on the hilltop.

This is the first time in the prehistory of Southern Africa that a senior
leader was so physically separated from his followers. This new spatial pattern is associated with class distinction, and it represents the origins of the
Zimbabwe culture.

Until now, Mapungubwe had been a rainmaking hill. By living on top, the
leader acquired the power of the place. His new location also emphasised the
link between himself, his ancestors and rainmaking. This link is an essential
characteristic of sacred leadership.

Southern terrace

The grey soil in front of the hill marks an extensive residential zone. The
deep hole, labelled as K8 on the excavation grid, reveals the great depth
of the deposit. Excavated in the 1980s, the stratigraphy here has helped
to determine the sequence of occupation in the whole site. Zone One,
at the bottom, was a sixth-century occupation by Early Iron Age farmers who used Mapungubwe Hill for rainmaking purposes. In Zone Two,
AD 1000–1220, when K2 was the capital, some K2 villagers lived at the
base of the hill. The relocation of the capital to Mapungubwe occurred in
Zone Three, AD 1220–1250. A horizon of burnt huts marks the transition

▲ Artist's reconstruction of Mapungubwe town centre

from Zone Two to Three, and it is possible that the people burnt the old village down to start the new capital afresh. Zone Four, AD 1250–1300, encompasses the decline of Mapungubwe in one interpretation, and its peak in another. This is the subject of on-going research.

Whatever the interpretation, Mapungubwe was only occupied as the capital for 50–80 years, less than half the duration of K2 – so the great depth of deposit on the Southern Terrace is the result of considerable human activity.

▲ Excavations of square K8, below Mapungubwe Hill. Note the stone foundations of grain bins, one above the other, and the depth of the deposit.

Court officials

Courts belonged to the leader of the settlement, but at Mapungubwe the sacred leader would seldom have been there, because he lived on the hill-top in ritual seclusion. We know from historical examples that a specially designated brother would instead have been in charge. Known as the 'little father' in some societies, this brother was the second most powerful man in the capital. This senior man would have had several messengers to summon people for a trial, as well as other officials to help run the court. His office was probably the stonewalled area against the large boulder next to the court. A terrace wall in front probably created a waiting place for people who had come to schedule a court case.

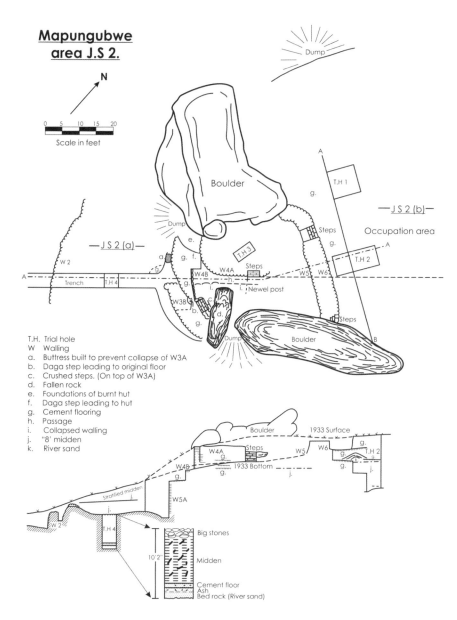

Mapungubwe area J.S 2.

N

0 5 10 15 20
Scale in feet

Dump

Boulder

Dump

— J S 2 (a) —

— J S 2 (b) —

Occupation area

T.H 1

g.

g.

Steps

A

A

T.H 2

W 2

A

Trench

T.H 4

e.

g. f.

a.

g.

W4B

W4A

Steps

Newel post

Steps

g.

h.

i.

i.

W5

W6

T.H 3

W3B

b.

c.

d.

g.

Dump

Boulder

B

Steps

T.H. Trial hole
W   Walling
a.   Buttress built to prevent collapse of W3A
b.   Daga step leading to original floor
c.   Crushed steps. (On top of W3A)
d.   Fallen rock
e.   Foundations of burnt hut
f.   Daga step leading to hut
g.   Cement flooring
h.   Passage
i.   Collapsed walling
j.   "8" midden
k.   River sand

Boulder

1933 Surface

W4A

Steps

W5

W6

g.

T.H 2

W4B

1933 Bottom

g.

g.

g.

j.

Stratified midden

j.

W5A

W 2

T.H 4

j.

10'2"

Big stones

Midden

Cement floor
Ash
Bed rock (River sand)

◄ Plan of the office of the 'little father' in charge of the court

▲ A 1930s photo shows stonewalling in front of the office. Note how the boulder fell and crushed the steps leading into the office area.

Occupation area

The senior man in charge of the court probably lived with his family in the small residential complex behind the stonewalled office. Excavations in the 1930s uncovered the remains of houses; the largest had been rebuilt at least three times and included a veranda with a small partition wall. The excavators left a witness section to show the successive floors. A small structure nearby may have been a store hut, while small stone circles supported grain bins. A midden full of animal bones still lies in the northern corner.

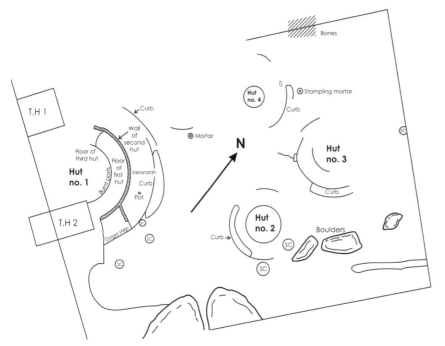

◀ Plan of the residential area behind the court complex

▲ The old photograph shows successive hut floors in the same area.

Plan of occupation area

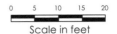

Scale in feet

T.H - Trial hole
S.C - Stone circle

Approaches

When Mapungubwe was the capital, there were four stairways up the hill. The main ascent led from the court to the narrow crack in the hillside. Pairs of holes drilled in the rock, underneath the modern ascent, once held poles to help form a stone stairway. Another stone stairway once led up the northern end of the hill. A large·block of sandstone has since broken off, but some of the drilled holes are still visible on the remaining rock. A third ascent starts about midway on the west side of the hill. This path connects the hilltop with one of the royal living areas. The final ascent leads up the eastern end of the hill. Stone walls at the top suggest that soldiers guarded this path. In later times, the soldiers were called the 'eye' of the king.

▼ Plan of Mapungubwe Hill showing the four main ascents

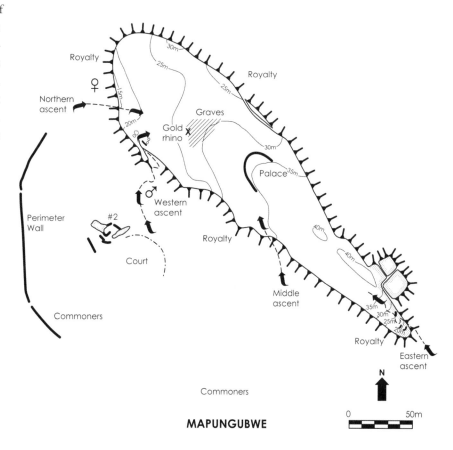

MAPUNGUBWE

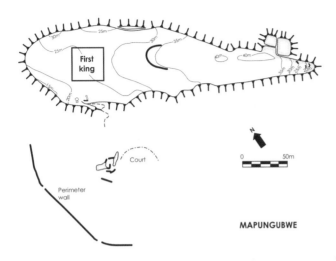

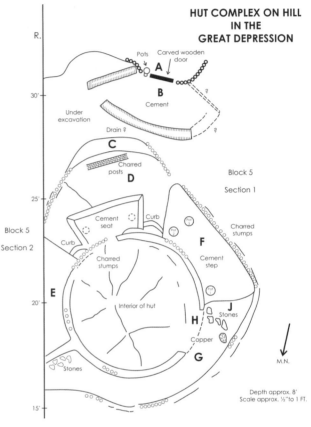

MAPUNGUBWE

First king

The main ascent leads up to the northwestern end of the hill, where excavations in the 1930s and 1980s uncovered a series of house floors. The deepest floor level dates to about AD 1220, and relates to the first sacred leader who lived on Mapungubwe Hill.

One unusual structure had a wide veranda with two fireplaces (called 'curbs') on either side of a seat. The veranda surrounded a small room with a clay floor so hard and well-made that early excavators called it 'cement'. Another house with the burnt remains of a carved wooden door stood opposite the fireplaces. If these structures followed the later Zimbabwe pattern, then the hut with the door was the king's own sleeping room, while the king's special diviner would have used the small hut with the exterior fireplaces. Somewhere nearby would have been an audience chamber where the king received visitors in a formal setting. Finally, the king's chief messenger would have kept an office towards the front where he could receive the visitors first.

▲ Clay structures in the first king's area
◀ Plan of Mapungubwe Hill showing where the first king lived

Stonewalling

The Zimbabwe culture is internationally known for impressive stonewalling. Few visitors realise, however, that the people at Mapungubwe pioneered the famous walling later used at Great Zimbabwe.

Three walling functions helped to facilitate sacred leadership and class distinction: prestige enclosures, hut terraces, and long boundaries. First and foremost, prestige walling provided ritual seclusion for the sacred leader. Here at Mapungubwe, retaining walls with irregular coursing in a vertical face form the palace front. Similar prestige walling characterises the office of the principal court official. In contrast, roughly piled terraces supported noble households. Other rough walling marks the front, western boundary of the town centre. This pattern was in place by AD 1250.

Different stonewalling at Mapungubwe:
◄ rough coursing of a terrace wall
▼ good coursing of the king's palace

First town

By AD 1250, when Mapungubwe was at its peak of power, some 5 000 people lived here. This population makes Mapungubwe Southern Africa's largest known settlement in its day, and its first town.

Commoners lived on the southern terrace and on the plateau to the north-east and east, between the sandstone hills. They would have been divided into residential units under the authority of family heads and headmen. Royalty, on the other hand, lived on the hut terraces that surrounded Mapungubwe Hill. Their location formed a protective circle around the king.

▶ Artist's reconstruction of the first town in southern Africa

Second king

By AD 1250, the king had shifted his official residence to the middle of the hill. The long arc of prestige walling there marks the first known palace of a king from the Zimbabwe culture.

Following the elite Zimbabwe settlement organisation, we would expect to find very few people in the palace. At the front would be the office of the king's senior messenger, whom visitors would have to see before approaching the king. The messenger, or his assistant, would take the visitors to the king's diviner who, with his special training, could tell if a person harboured evil. The guides would then take visitors to the official audience chamber to meet the king. This large structure was usually divided in two, so that visitors were separated from the king and his entourage. The king slept in a small hut (with a wooden door) in a secret location. In the back section of the palace lived one or two of the king's youngest wives. Their location was also supposed to be secret. Nearby was the national ritual area, where some aspects of rainmaking took place. This ritual area would have space for several people as well as a place for storing the national drum and other sacred objects.

The physical separation of the king from his subjects was an outward expression of sacred leadership. The king would have also been separated through the formal behaviour surrounding his office. For example, people

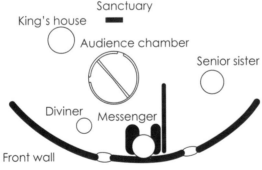

▲ Idealised plan of a Zimbabwe-culture palace

◀ The terrace wall of the first palace

◀ A board game played by men on rock
in front of the palace

43

probably knelt in his presence, spoke to him through an intermediary, rather than directly, and referred to him metaphorically as the 'mountain'.

A special male entourage of soldiers, musicians and praise singers would have surrounded the king. Some features in front of the palace indicate their presence. A few game boards, for example, were pecked into the sandstone bedrock. Throughout Africa, only men played this kind of game, and so the boards probably marked the location of soldiers who guarded the palace.

According to sixteenth century records, musicians played mbiras and xylophones at a chief's place, near the front door, to add dignity to the surroundings.

On formal occasions a praise singer would precede the king, shouting honorific titles and other compliments. Because the king's actions were ritualised, if he so much as sneezed, everyone would know within minutes.

Some of these praise singers, musicians and soldiers would have had homes elsewhere in the capital, but some would have stayed on the hill. Many deep holes and circular grooves in the sandstone supported the posts of houses that probably sheltered this entourage.

◄ A circular groove in the sandstone of the hilltop used to help anchor a house.

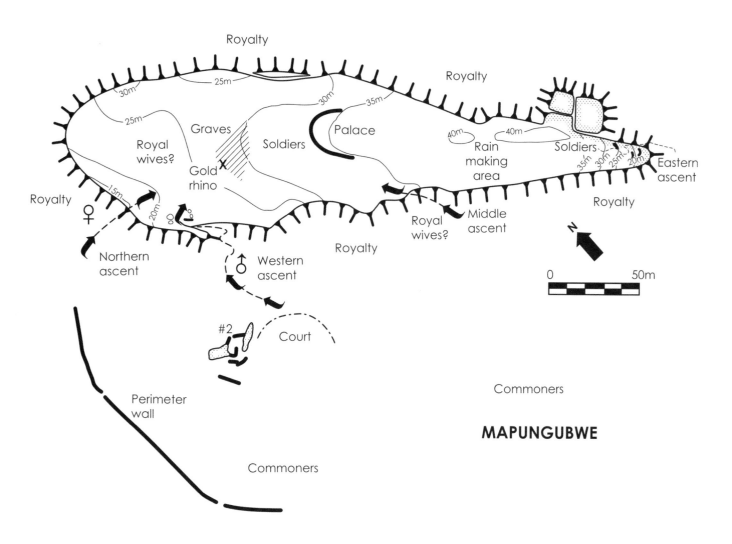

Royalty

Royalty

30m
25m
25m
30m
35m
30m

Royal wives?

Graves

Soldiers

Palace

Gold rhino

40m
40m

Rain making area

Soldiers

35m 30m 25m 20m

Eastern ascent

15m

Royalty

♀

20m
⚲

Northern ascent

♂

Western ascent

Royalty

Royal wives?

Middle ascent

Royalty

N

0   50m

Northern ascent

#2

Court

Commoners

MAPUNGUBWE

Perimeter wall

Commoners

▲ Plan of Mapungubwe Hill showing locations of different features and activities

Royal wives

Throughout Southern Africa, wives were an avenue to success and status, and the number of wives was a direct reflection of a man's wealth and political power. The king at Mapungubwe would therefore have had many, and more than any other man in the kingdom. Leaders of equivalent status in historic times had as many as 100.

Most of the king's wives would have lived in a special area of their own outside the palace. The senior wife would have been in charge and the official liaison with the king. The northwest end, where the first king stayed, has yielded the only lower grindstone on the hill, and this female artefact suggests that this may have been the royal wives' area. The debris from copper smelting has also been found here, and, as at K2, copper working may have been associated with a female residential zone.

Not all the king's wives would necessarily have stayed in the capital. As part of the political system, some would have lived in subsidiary settlements under the protection of petty chiefs. These distant wives helped to maintain a network of alliances, and when the king went on an inspection tour, he would always have a wife to look after him.

Royal cemetery

Excavations in the 1930s uncovered a major cemetery between the women's area and the palace. This cemetery contained 23 graves: most bodies were buried in a flexed position on their sides, but three were different. The first, No. 14, probably a woman, was buried in a sitting posture facing west: she wore at least 100 gold bangles around her ankles, and there were over 12 000 gold beads and 26 000 glass beads in the grave. Burial No. 10 was a tall middle-aged man, also sitting up facing west: he wore a necklace of gold beads and cowrie shells, and there were some objects covered in gold foil in the grave, one resembling a crocodile. The third, known as the 'original gold burial', was also a male, but his burial posture is unknown: he was buried with a wooden headrest and three objects made from gold foil – a bowl, a sceptre (probably a knobkerrie) and a rhino. At least two more rhinos came from the graveyard, but it is not known what grave they came from.

These grave goods have now become world famous. In recognition of their importance, the South African Heritage Resources Agency has declared them a National Treasure.

Other than these grave goods, the amount of wealth in the cemetery was not great. Traditionally, death is the leveller in most of southern Africa, and what wealth there is should be spent on the funeral. The goods in the three special graves, however, were clearly related to status. People of high stature, we know, were usually buried in a cattle kraal. Considering that soil was purposefully deposited to make the cemetery, it may have had a fence surrounding it to resemble a kraal.

▲ The sceptre from the original gold burial

◀ The royal grave area on the hilltop, in an old photograph

Golden rhinos

Because the K2 and Mapungubwe people developed a cultural system that lasted for several hundred years, it is possible to use historic data to interpret the symbolism of the rhino. Of the two kinds in southern Africa, the white rhino is relatively docile and harmless, but the black rhino is just the opposite. It is known for its dangerous behaviour, unpredictability, power and solitary life. These were also attributes of sacred leaders.

Furthermore, a black rhino will destroy a bush or termite mound in great fury, stamping the ground and tossing soil and leaves into the air. This action is similar to a special dance that Zimbabwe culture leaders performed on the graves of their ancestors. Because of this similarity, the name for a black rhino in the Shona and Venda languages (*chipembere*) is a cognate for the name of the dance. For all these reasons, the black rhino was an appropriate symbol of leadership.

▲ Two of the golden rhinos from the royal cemetery: probably symbols of leadership

Gold working

Arab authors such as al-Masudi mention the Sofala gold trade in the tenth century, and at that time most of southern Africa's gold was exported. It is noteworthy that Mapungubwe has produced the earliest finished objects in the interior of southern Africa: gold now had an indigenous value, and was not simply a means to aquire wealth.

Gold was processed with the same technology as copper. It was first melted in a small clay crucible in a clay furnace to produce nodules that were then made into beads, formed into wire or beaten into sheets. The bowl from the 'original gold burial' is a typical example of sheets tacked onto a wooden core.

Evidence of gold working, such as the crucibles, has been found in the back, private section of a few later palaces. It is not yet clear, however, whether these finds mark true industrial areas or whether a small amount was melted only for symbolic purposes.

◀ The golden bowl from the original gold burial

First state

Mapungubwe's size, about 5 000 people, correlates well with historical examples of capitals at the top of a five-level hierarchy of leadership: (1) family heads, (2) headmen, (3) petty chiefs, (4) senior chiefs, and (5) the king. This kind of hierarchy is necessary for the administration of many people spread over a wide area. Indeed, all known examples, such as the Zulu, Venda and Ngwato states, covered about 30 000 square kilometres – the size of present-day Swaziland or Lesotho.

Mapungubwe pottery, developed at Mapungubwe, appears to have changed into another style after Mapungubwe was abandoned. The Mapungubwe style therefore dates to a very short period, and its distribution probably reflects the size of the kingdom. Significantly, the pottery covers about 30 000 square kilometres. If the pottery style represents a single political entity, then Mapungubwe was the first state in Southern Africa.

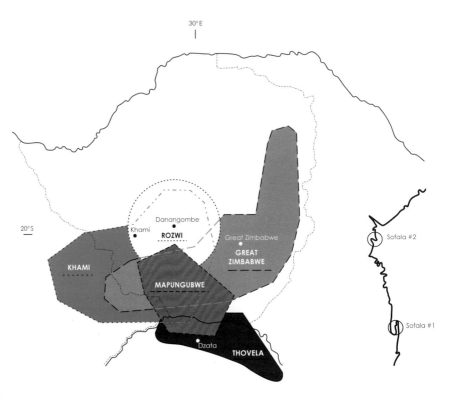

▲ Map showing the large area under the control of Mapungubwe

Internal trade and contacts

Various resources were scattered over the Mapungubwe state and neighbouring areas. Copper and gold, for example, occurred in Botswana, South Africa and Zimbabwe. Salt was a natural product of the Makgadikgadi Pans in Botswana, while ancient tin mines exist at Rooiberg in South Africa.

In addition, the presence of foreign pottery shows that there was contact with other areas. Styles characteristic of Eiland to the south and Toutswe to the west are both present in deposits at Mapungubwe. This pottery may have come from marriage alliances, rather than trade, but it nevertheless shows the extensive network centred on Mapungubwe.

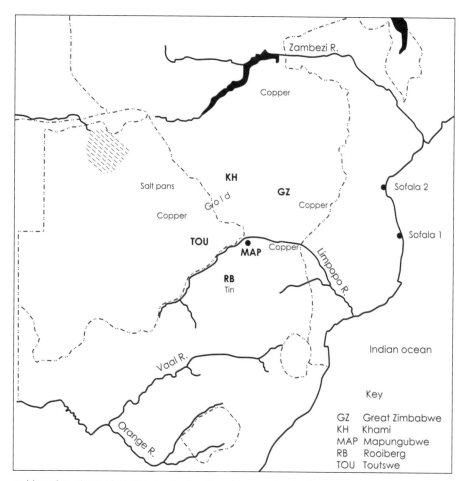

▲ Map of southern Africa showing the location of important natural resources

External trade

The economic base of Mapungubwe included the Indian Ocean gold and ivory trade, as it had before with K2. Mapungubwe people continued to trade for glass beads from India and South East Asia. In fact, archaeologists have recovered a huge number: over 26 000 just from burial No. 14 on the hilltop. Many beads, incidentally, are small and regular, which makes them suitable for sewing complex patterns onto cloth, and not just simple strings.

◀ Clay spindle whorls used to spin cotton grown in the basin

◄ Chinese celadon imported as part of the Indian Ocean trade; probably a gift to the king

Clay spindle whorls appear for the first time in the interior at Mapungubwe and show that Mapungubwe people were making their own cloth. The cotton was probably indigenous, but the craft was introduced from the Swahili coast where it was an important industry.

Chinese celadon, a blue-green glazed stoneware, has been found in the palace. Generally, glazed pottery was not desirable locally because it was unsuitable for cooking: local earthenware served this purpose better. Following custom, the celadon in the palace would have been a gift to the king for allowing foreigners to trade.

Commoners

At the peak of Mapungubwe's importance, many people lived on the land as well as in the capital. In fact, populations had grown to the point where there were four times as many people in the basin as in the Zhizo period.

People living next to the floodplains would have concentrated on cultivation, while other homesteads away from the river would probably have been more concerned with cattle. All, however, still organised their homesteads according to the Central Cattle Pattern. This continuity contrasts with the new elite pattern at the capital, and provides further evidence for class distinction. People using the Central Cattle Pattern were commoners.

▼ Map showing distribution of Mapungubwe-period settlements

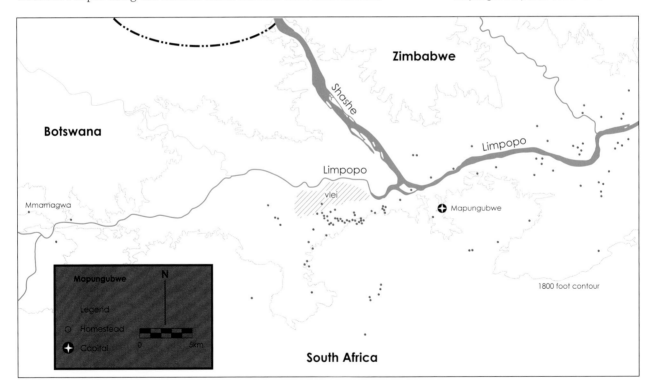

Climatic change

The good climate that characterised the region during K2 times came to an end because of the spread of the Little Ice Age. Cold conditions appear to have started at about AD 1300 throughout southern Africa. Because of the previously warm conditions, the initial impact would have been particularly severe. For agriculture in the basin, the sudden and severe impact would have been disastrous. For example, flooding at the wrong time for three to five successive years would have destroyed the agricultural system. At about AD 1300 the basin was abandoned, and Mapungubwe people scattered to the northwest and south. They never regrouped at a large capital.

The political successor to Mapungubwe, of course, was Great Zimbabwe. Some Mapungubwe royalty may have participated in the growth of Great Zimbabwe, but, as the ceramic evidence shows, the people at Great Zimbabwe were a different group.

Great Zimbabwe was on the fringe of the Mapungubwe state, and the people there would have witnessed the rise of Mapungubwe. When Great Zimbabwe replaced Mapungubwe as the regional centre of power, it adopted the new elite settlement pattern, as well as class distinction and sacred leadership. Great Zimbabwe was therefore Mapungubwe's cultural successor, too.

ICON, KHAMI AND VENDA

Icon and Khami occupations

A warm climatic pulse at about AD 1350 made the basin habitable again to farmers. At this time, the first Sotho-Tswana people moved from East Africa into southern Africa. Icon pottery, named after the farm where it was first found, marks the distribution of the earliest Sotho-Tswana in the region. Most homesteads were not sited near the floodplains, either because the people were unaware of the basin's agricultural history, or because elephant herds had returned.

Fifty years later, Shona-speaking people from Zimbabwe (associated with Khami pottery) moved into the basin and lived along the edge of the flood-plains. Prestige stonewalling marks the location of royal headmen and chiefs. One chief lived on a rocky outcrop on Den Staat, and two headmen stayed near Mapungubwe Hill. The hill itself was never reoccupied.

▲ The remains of a Khami-period palace in the basin

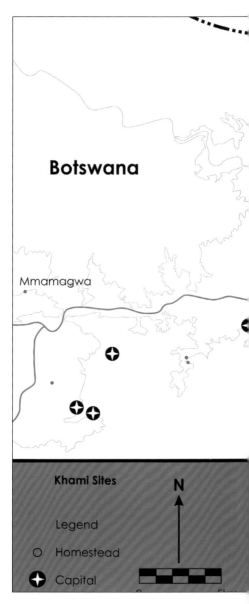

Botswana

Mmamagwa

▶ Khami sites

Khami Sites

N

Legend

O   Homestead

✦   Capital

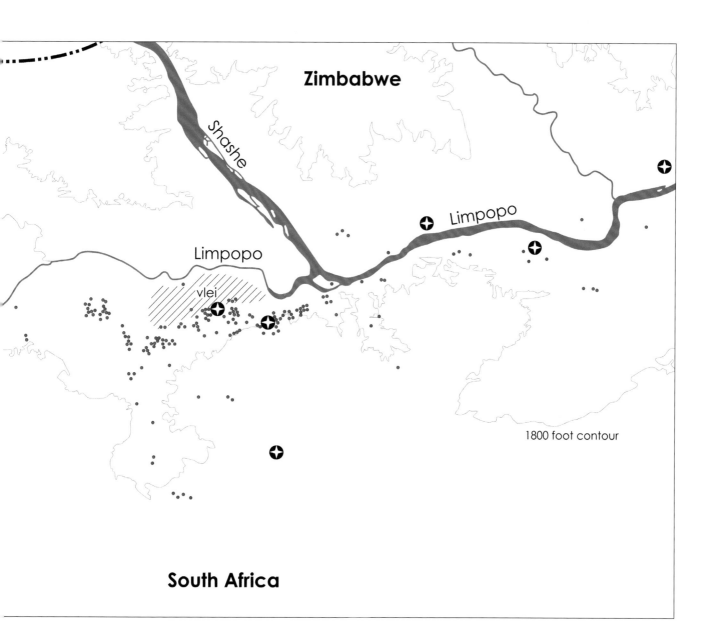

Zimbabwe

Shashe

Limpopo

Limpopo

vlei

1800 foot contour

South Africa

Origins of the Venda

The Zimbabwe culture first developed at Mapungubwe continues today among the Venda people, and so their origins in South Africa are linked to the story of Mapungubwe. Venda oral traditions present three successive cultural influences: (1) Ngona groups who were found there, (2) Shona groups from Zimbabwe (such as the Lembethu and Mbedzi) who were independent but equal to each other, and (3) Singo groups from Zimbabwe who conquered the country. For many years, some scholars believed that the Singo were the true Venda. Recent research helps to clarify this question.

We now know that Shona-speaking chiefdoms, based on sacred leadership and class distinction, moved south of the Limpopo between about AD 1400 and 1450. Their capitals were all the same size, supporting the tradition that the chiefs were politically equal. These Shona chiefdoms (with Khami pottery) incorporated earlier Sotho-Tswana people (Icon pottery). After about 100 years, they had created the Venda language (associated with Letaba pottery). Later, at about AD 1690, the Singo (who had been part of the important Rozwi dynasty in Zimbabwe) moved south and conquered most of Venda. Thus, Venda culture and language came into existence before the Singo movement.

Venda occupation

Depending on environmental conditions, among other things, Venda chiefdoms occupied the basin from time to time. European glass beads, such as blue hexagonals, date most of the capitals to the nineteenth century. Uncoursed walling with loopholes for guns also characterises Venda capitals at this time.

As a result of military tensions, the organisation of Venda capitals was slightly different from the Zimbabwe pattern. The sacred leader lived on top of a hill, or on the upper slopes, while royal wives lived on hut terraces somewhat lower down, rather than to the side where they would be vulnerable to attack. The main court at the bottom separated the chief's wives from commoners in the capital. Several good examples of nineteenth-century capitals are on record in Botswana and Zimbabwe as well as in South Africa.

▼ Venda walling in the basin; note the loopholes.

CONCLUSION

The importance of the Mapungubwe Cultural Landscape to the early history of southern Africa is enormous. It was here that social, cultural and political developments led to the first complex society in southern Africa. Although Mapungubwe people eventually abandoned the landscape, the new type of society continued on at Great Zimbabwe and other places in Botswana, Mozambique and Zimbabwe, as well as South Africa.

The initial developments were due to the impact of long-distance trade on the one hand and intensive agriculture on the other. Agricultural produce and trade wealth made it possible for large populations and formal social classes to develop.

Trade and agriculture also contributed to the rise of civilisations else-where, and so the development of complex society at Mapungubwe is of international interest. Since the development of Mapungubwe only began 1 000 years ago, we hope that present and future research will help to clarify the origins of civilisation in antiquity.

* * *

Before the 1990s, few people in South Africa had heard of Mapungubwe. Now it is an increasingly important part of the national consciousness about the African past. Indeed, one of the gold rhinos from Mapungubwe has become a national icon, symbolising past achievements. What is more, the government has established a prestigious medal known as The Order of Mapungubwe for South Africa's most distinguished citizens. Thus, the achievements of the past still have resonance today.

FURTHER READING

Bullock, C. 1927. *The Mashona.* Cape Town: Juta.

Fouche, L. (ed.) 1937. *Mapungubwe: Ancient Bantu Civilisation on the Limpopo.* Cambridge: Cambridge University Press.

Gardner, G.A. 1963. *Mapungubwe: Vol. 2.* Pretoria: J.L. van Schaik.

Huffman, T.N. 1996. *Snakes & Crocodiles: Power and Symbolism in Ancient Zimbabwe.* Johannesburg: Witwatersrand University Press.

Leslie, M. & Maggs, T. (eds.) 2000. *African Naissance: The Limpopo Valley 1000 Years Ago.* South African Archaeological Society Goodwin Series 8.

Meyer, A. 1998. *The Archaeological Sites of Greefswald: Stratigraphy and Chronology of the Sites and a History of Investigations.* Pretoria: University of Pretoria.

Mönnig, H.O. 1967. *The Pedi.* Pretoria: J.L. van Schaik.

Stayt, H.A. 1931. *The Bavenda.* Oxford: Oxford University Press for the International African Institute.

Voigt, E.A. 1983. *Mapungubwe: An Archaeo-geological Interpretation of an Iron Age Community.* Pretoria: Transvaal Museum.

GLOSSARY

artefact: something made by humans, e.g. tools, artworks

bride price: cattle or money given by a bridegroom to his bride's family

Central Cattle Pattern: design of homestead around cattle kraal, typical of the Eastern Bantu-speaking people in southern Africa

cistern: water-storage tank

cognate: related/meaning the same

confluence: point where rivers flow together

craton: unbroken /unfaulted part of the earth's crust

cupule: cup-shaped hole in the ground

dolly hole: used as mortar for grinding grain or ore, or as a socket for a wooden house post

dyke: wall-like body of rock

Eastern Bantu: group of related languages of Eastern Africa

escarpment: steep ridge created by erosion

fluvial terrace: 'step' eroded by river

magma: molten rock

mbira: thumb piano

midden: rubbish heap

Middle Iron Age: from AD 900–1300

monsoon: seasonal winds of the Indian Ocean, blowing ships to the East in [months] and back towards Africa in [months]

spindle whorls: part of rod used to make thread from fibres

stratigraphy: a vertical section through the earth showing the relative positions of human artefacts and therefore the chronology of successive levels of occupation

topography: surface features of a region

Zimbabwe culture: archaeological name for societies in southern Africa who used stonewalled palaces for ritual seclusion of sacred leaders